SCINTILLA

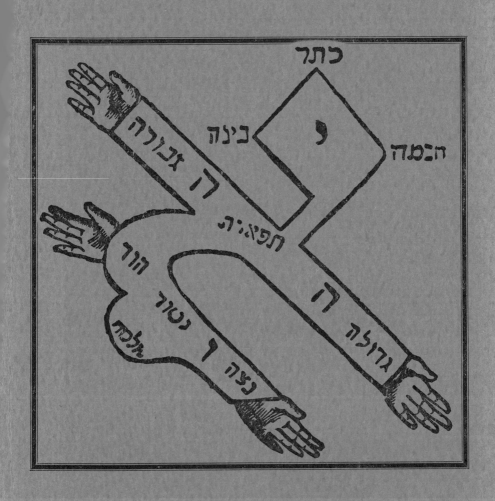

JACK HIRSCHMAN

SCIN TILLA

JACK HIRSCH MAN

TREE
BOOKS
1971

© Jack Hirschman 1971
published by Christopher Books
1819 Sycamore Canyon Road
Santa Barbara, California 93103

ISBN 0-87922-000-7
Library of Congress Card 77-168539

SCINTILLA

CHILD

See there is another   and another Ah   they move how fast
they run about is it fire   it is like wild   fire they are little
stars upon the ground   so that my master   and I lept
from the high place where it was lonely   and dark   fell once
upon again back to the black   movements of the earth   took
turns in the fat old book of   the night   dancing letters
happy in small   print the whole mass   of scintillations

DILDO

In quiet despair of a cycle   in cool exhaustion in the night
     of Angels everywhere in Paris in London in New York   in-
side the In of the Inner at the point of black   humor and the
travesties   of betrayal and sell of wartold lies returning
to mouths eating the crows   of Van Goghs purity anonymous
ecstacies of wooden   hair and Zimpandu barked   through
the only bony christ concretely   hung around one's own neck
     in the lap of Maria strung up on the negatives   of the
astrologies spurting   scorpion wads of counterfeit paradox
     I conjure you Dildo   out of the dark of this bark of Death
turning over   each moments decay lovely   soil in the gut
met in the spit of the eyeballs coming   to meet one on the
humiliated street of this night limned   with leathery halo fan-
tasies   searching one wrist of a red   rod one son of a nun
     one curse to be blessed one   finger of tendresse longing to
be   a boys whittle usage   of flute in the tough fenderloved
last gasps   of a politic desolate as a couple   of broadsides
slapped against the hips   of a revolution turned into granite
mass with all the quick juice gone   from the two of us and
all   the kingdom come shot out of the motels eyes knocking
about   in the pockets with lost marbles   Old Cob I make
you   no new woman but myself appended awake with the
poems strapped round your deep body   artificial Jerusalem
with its cruelty of theaters   meshed with wild fences and the
stocking of Zero each line   of this new man and woman shall
     with tall and straight branching of our small forest
loyalties   fall from the sky fill the woman come upon me
with the tree story   unscrolled from the biblical root

9

FAULT

Black gold vein streak   you break my   cock you eat   my
blood black flood my ark my steel now   yours my knot our
jah   one gut string blue one   note throughout   a pride
of two   chaingang song shouts the house gone down   in
blooming truth in here   where I give up my name my blame
   turns gold called Jack   is black and jew

INITIAL

Softly let me   begin with outside   help with outside in
another season   laying the assassination to   one side plac-
ing the private nightmare   to the other   standing between
making the sign of   crossing under the only star   be Are

CYCLE

I return to the tender   lonely streets of the nights   small
vision of boyhood growing   a friend the shadows are shoes
   too large as if having outlived one marriage   I stand at the
end of the law with wife and children contained   the corner
erupting with   strollers passing among the first   movie-
houses of dreams   first painting of a nude stretched   upon
gentian velvet in a little shopwindow sitting on the railway   in
Poe   Park watching the skirts whirl the shadows of legs
   slowly branching against the dark sky of mind what am I
doing here   Im thirtyfour not seventeen   have stopped
reading books am ashen   within with decay and war crumbles
      get out of this hopeless borough   old banalities go down
go down   to the man size dark Manhattan   the chains of
womanly nays   at the statue of Dante in Lincoln Park
   this too has been razed   a couple of hells sweet law smooch-
ing seventy yearold   lushes on a bench twilight she turns
observing me observing   my own birth crying out   what
are you looking at you cocksucker   her mouth the degraded
truth in the window on the Avenue   of the Americas beside

10

the vanity mirror became deaths vampiric skull   there is the
green   edition of Fragments my thin first book   of poems
my old eyes Zero   cynically in on with this fierce gaze blazing   down love   with this black fire

REMINGTON NOISELESS

The strange force of my father   breaking up through the
ground of this quaking California   feeling   the miles between us tenderly now to know   we must hold to these
shulamiths closely small boys of the lonesome   brotherhood
trying to   befriend the friend lost when we   won the war
down here   I have lived out the act of my old man   ascend-
ing the steps of the crowd of the child rising ego   broken with
him into a hundred   demagogues walked through the 72
     circles of blear and ditched   ruts of the eyes in hell reached
     the synagogue nose-down like a stuka in the flesh of the
night mare   no one can escape   so he just hands me these
words in a way   no film can show praise   the distance
between us as I   pass them to you   praise what pulls up
in front of your face   all flows

MOBILE

Incidentally the center is   everywhere now yesterday was
     the sun the day before   yesterday a man   walked around
and paradoxically take pride in the facts   of life of death   all
the chairs and tables inbetween you used   to call a man
comes in sits down   there is no one to serve him   in another
time   I would have   begged you shove a loaf of bread
through   the poem to feed him   now can only say in this
event there is a   deeply religious conversation   himself
and a chair is having

NOW

Now this contempt makes   such oceanic plums   such soft
indignities always in the act of   falling and rising like hope

11

for an end turning the corner blushingly   violet leaving the
lips   empty a tit of political headline a paranoic slice of
swissed   cheese she was emerging slowly from darkness to
stand   in the flanks of the little street   a dingy apocalypse
setting a strand   straight   a tottle of the gas of a hat wanting   a limp or deaf eye or be struck   down dumb so the
others would talk   with their fingers   he was what   the
bloody blunderer cut out   for us between the thighs   a
stash of beard the hooks of   a fix of stymie   each moments
egg a brood of revenges under the fingernails   until we all
fill   up with rods inside

SVELTE

One wrist between you   both one slavic   streak lightning
shows your blond her black   hair a moment before   going
out in the night of fur and suede   braided together   one
style one solitude in sheer   stockings buckled tight   one
laughter intimately clear   cheekbones meeting   at the chin
of a rich thunder

DEAN

Through you through   the middle eye   star of false light
    our photographic   dark raum the other side   to this
clearing this long   standing wood   this tree   brother of
solitude and regret   thin brother spending your split throughout   the cafes of Europe   camerado of taste flashing from
collage to collage   deathbearing seed of the steeple crying
mad boy   behind a mask of infamous fame   damned to be
observed by billboards   to be rumored among gumwrapper
    in the gutter   actor of passives   director of volts   my
lost sensitivity   friend looking over his first   lovelost and
turning   shyly into   whatever is French understands you
young decay   celibate journey   hermit thin way through
snake money Isidore slash Ducasse   who flows by withdraw-
ing   95 miles an hour on the San   Diego freeway at dawn
    ephemerica   high up the hills   down deep the steps
    cabin of chopped lightnings   distance between history and
beauty   closing with the wobbling rock of your night   a

12

bike rumbles out   of a postage stamp of Einstein   entering
my senses   go from cycle to cycle   these bandage worn
bleeding roses to bind

CREELEY

At night I walk   around the cell   sitting still beside you
    it is all there is   to do at twelve   years old my voice
       broken into the second throat   of confirmation young and
old   friend of a son of a son   means names and names
    preserve   the word running out of this instrument moving
       west to east   across the lands mourning song how slowly
how lonely how john   the dues collector   from within a
world of so many spending   whores to make   sensitive vi-
brations for when day and night both   are dragged out
beaten   a clubby fascist long enough   now I be a master-
ing   slave to   the rose is   the crossing   her man the
sea   in my name

MEMOIRE: DIANE

Her hair the burning   leaves of the   night stem pommelled
to a darkness faint   with nibbles of her lip   drowned sleep
       the tips of cigarets   her eyes the meadow run   through
and through with cockcrow bursting into the golden   gibberish
of this black and blue dawn   with her long stretch of gear
sensitive depravity frill of the parasite   tit pulsing against
    my wall almost a wail a siren   of frail   schoolgirls

GLYPH

Now slowly soul   now twotiming company   rise   to this
occasion of his eyes   in death blazing   his curls waving
       onto the land tongue of my tongue   intertwining   death
and this sentence that goes on   dribbling   away into the
grey of his second   living father of my hearts crown   child
of my courage   biff visionary of the ways of the interknit

13

sweater of our families   a fagend in the mouth   a black
in the eye   mother and daughter on each of his paws   the
honey poem   of his excruciation

EMBLEM

When I was asked to be   present at this future   now I
feared for my life used   to be easy   and now goes simply
in whispers   leaning against the waves   somewhere away
and where   there are clearings binding us in this sweet
fanatical revolution   a work of art botched and terrifying
    with beauty falling   face down in the blown out rice paddy
of the face   is the real   fiction we are bending over backwards to proclaim   what I give name   the cruel poem I
reach down to tear up   by roots   kiss in into the open
air   is mother and child and the bird   breaks from the
socket of buddhas   eye flies back into the black   blinding
river

ERRINNERRUNGG

Smells off her loveliness   reminding my body   of the onion
skins stroked with all densities   of erhebungs between
thousands of miles three hours after   for the street she comes
    from unstable books nerve endings endlessly   shaking a
student out in the   morning flap of an ancient flag   without
as yet and perhaps   never will the middle   of the story
find a pillow   under the dreams head   with hair long
enough to play east and west   between thighs interchangeable
body of berry to rise   in brown ease and a dark   constric-
tion of a chord shuddering   deep into the tubes scooped out
    and left is this silent volume   birthing this   rapid wing
bleeding   out into the open   air and embrasure   of your
eyelid hovering   over all the notes torn   into bits of rain
    bow linking all   the armed scores the fiumed

LINT

Mind a shambles they   have hung up my balls in   but who
    but things appear never the same   way twice in front of
me   each time I look over there   will all the be all   of a
sensitive poetry be   unfolding this cruel crop   of magic
    being played on the worst   organs left now the dice are
Ten   the figurine of the rabbi has turned   his back I didn't
do it it   happened completely at the mercy   of word things
violent musicks done to   self is   sanity is   chaos where
nothing fits everything plays   with itself within   a sitdown
    strike for stillness

CYCLOPS

Now I walk with   the tiger of my soul stroking   his growls
letting them out through the bars   of Jerusalem at the end
    beginning over and over The Name   never finishing off
the mountains around where he leaps in the night   ocean
where he breathes his fierce mists I tell you the passion   is
true and clear   through the bones the eyes burn with whirl-
winds of indifferent   rainbows his teeth every jail set before
me   his tough fall of paw solid earth   wondering under
massive yet here   in this small form made big   with
thunder for having lived through the cycle   of woman for
having arrived at the lion time I clash   down on knees animal
brother I rise   up at the flash of the night

LAUTRE AMONT

I am exploding dog   went to Montivideo to find   the scowl
of my ancestor   no book can help   skull is the Globe
Theater of Athanasius Kircher   the cycle turned over and an
empty   blackleather jacket fell out   her anger at my sperm
took itself   out in my face the night I am driving   is passing through my fingers   Wall covered with yesterdays fade-
out posters   her garters loved   every mouth coming to lap

at history   the repeated wear and tear   of a monoto-
nous war on my eyelids   going to sleep sick of seeing
words choking on pup sounds popular tunes   TEXACO
gas war at two   oclock theres no time for time   once again
footage is streaming   down the canyons with the story   of
everything   is a car on its nose   space technologists come
out of beer cans   announcing escrow   heroin is behind me
wearing   a dildo   I can find nothing underneath   in the
silent moviehouse on Fairfax my daughter and I   watch
silence for three hours   the answer is in the Pacific at dawn
I am always sleeping intention of the government is to make
the world over a shabby greytweed bone   dreaming
kabbala would lead me to   you its led me to   you not
enough money in the pocket   juice in the machine did Gomez
tell the truth when he said   he saw him in Bolivia what
did Hefner mean up in Toronto in 1934   I would have been
one year old long dream not to be put down   but picked up
from time to time and smoked in the punctuated   musicality
of forgetfulness   she shot down twelve   if this is a game
or something why   are the latest reports from Utah negative
who the hell asked   Brewster his opinion anyway imme-
diately translated into Chinese   the entire earthly natural
dark man hand   at hip with her with whom   is womb and
there it is they are in   shoot your self at this point   if only
hed let me   for seven days I dug   every grave in Prague
no dice   fuck it the code was evil anyway spit went into
orbit around all beards   the same old scissors wherever you
go   the girl the rain and me   automatic handling of a
bunch of achtungs wrapped in tinfoil   poor angry   black
man at my window her mesh   stockings the color of   our
infinite humor from 1968 to 1929   when the riots began
from the south will you   stop it already well have the killer
by midnight folded over her arm   all drugs have been
made standard   press that one Jerusalem   secret police say
theyve got him hold up   in Islington the girl of eighteen rung
me up couldnt stop talking   wore a little   dickie confessed
nothing the Goodyear zeppelin glide   over Venice   said his
name was   Harloff while trying to escape   longhair looked
like   a rat

16

STROKES

The only thing   happening is   the sea at two   of death
at three or ten in anarchy   leaving the tree leaving   it all
burning behind without song or style mind   of city man and
woman   blind to the round power   smithereened all turned
to braille gone   to hell of grass and here am   I dance
by the   oceanic turbine   in the minds dead spring gone
des   troyed on the sand   hung by thumbs upon numbers
punished by headlines   crawling away from   her wave to
lie down the plum dark spread   fierce flower my love returning   the gaze fix for fix   these asterisks of domination
dawn of the limp stem with eros run out   of reeds to dip into
the pith of the fruit writing kiss in a broken rhyme
stands still and hums   hand scoops up jerusalem   running
out   bleeding grain by grain

SELAH

Black mother madame   of mind my passion   black biblical
nook in the spread on night   under the white mask   freeze
black jesus to all my christ   black thighbone and common
sense the seasons eat as the famine of the land is   deep
washed and licked cats in the screaming   sleep all our fires
who taught me the wrong road rightly   crawl in the gutter
home to the backsided slaps for the good   measure of keeping trim this slim primordial   girl remembrance of the inside
of your   black   brassiere the stifling smell of flesh in the
winter cold   sullen lazy movements of heels across the lino-
leum squares   Death you gave and give   and more life
in the ironic   kickback smile and spoon raised   higher than
the fist the soup pouring   golems into the nasty bowls
black fire all the way summer under armpits dream   the other
forest   Zaddiks in the trees children walking upsidedown
Ayins   thrust in   I do   I wept then was married to
black   was born to me   this jew with the world with the
round world flat   on his head   praying each step singing
under the breath of the cold   dancing behind eyelids
gazing after who but Thee backside who but   Thee   would
understand be   understood in the eyes of   if Thou wouldst

17

turn   burn those gutterfilthy   songs out of my eyes cut
   the mesh stocking of fantasy tear   my garterbelt off beat
me dumb animal lick   this ghetto charred and running
allover your inner lips   I can put my finger on   my tongue
on delicate   and me a spider me a wasp   honey bee fly
honey be my eyes   flung out of your hands black   susans
   trucking through my nights   tall thighs turning over senti-
mental mush under such fierce dominion   the soul of my
whore the old hooker shuck   who keeps the kitty is   why
we are already   old and born that way   chillin   born
that flesh back movement   sunday spanking shoes on the pave-
ment dying   in need of him who was a good riddance   sis-
ter   you come ups here and take   my arm mother you come
ups here and take   my other now   this is my war
song this is my cry hell   you are the magic   diablos
and   tarotcards   Moon   you   be   twofaced   me   one
for the blue boy   one for the daddy   fragments all told
mosaic table of the law of   our black spring and fall to
return he does The Bird wakes up   the lungs with music
run down man   spent and dead nihil   revolutionary of
nothing but the songs   of black money sounds restoreth my
   nothing while you come you run   into me the big wagon of
my baggage of three   my heavy load I fill with names with
games of chance   music cry my fists out beat   the wall out
   my already beaten in cage   you rage your age you are
   age time yours and mine   both of us and all old and young
in this   turning   when the sky give out when the meadow-
lark   song didnt we   come didnt we   come home finally
huddling under the El holding hands   the war she is   never
ending with tall black head   lines dropping out the back
   of the trucks on the last cobbles   to kick

POWER

Ancient beside you   ancient as in archaic or simple   beginning steady rising and falling of   breath in breathing   out
the old crumbling mind is into   the great body you   are still
older and more   still more   anarchic in your tides of
old flames all my rain   streams pouring down into this
   one dwindling blue in December   beside who is source of
all   electric the power surpassed for   older and more des-
tructive   utter and complete submission   fundamental turbine no remorse all tear   death split   I am dead without

18

who has with   you have white under   sucked the shem
    ham for   ash of the spark   sucked the exilic   Kid
Dybbuk home

AVELAVAL

And if I blame what   is there to blame   what   is there
when the matter is a joke on so many   lips and Ive heard a
man   say its a woman and another a cigaret   and still
another   the left lobe of my back side kiss it   or him or
what   you will and still   you will this through all and me
nothing   no matter whatever be said   only this moment
this no other in which   my head is drenched with   trancing
in which not even the dance knows   what I do comes out so
    clearly obscure   is called good bad or   as you like it
doesnt matter I know   in this fiction with this fiction this
    bitch of nothing I have only   exhaustedly desperately burn-
ingly futilely and most   oh more most importantly mindlessly
full   of you   lived

ASA

I nested a man in my mouth   breeds me to the night music
mare   between us these reeds of a war   of words were
forever slashing   he grows as I fall   he wears the dunce-
cap of innocence now we lock horns   in the gun sighted forest
where the animals   verge   we branch all over the plot of
this poverty   struck globe   his shambles mine hung up in
the sun blue aiees   in the moon mother in the moon   we are
two   halves of a head   broke   down the middle by a
whirl   wind of a distant victory landing on our feet   with
a sigh at the bottom of all   riding the street lined with trash
bites and dead reactions   the words exhausted the inner bones
of the drama gone   flat   universal cracked at the joints
these letters and numbers abbreviated   leaps of the hope of a
blood to walk high cambric north on   the dark mountain wood
    setting trees aflame in his eyes bent forever   on a spark
and a poem   mother your simple light song framed   by the
deer where we stand   looking through you undresses itself of
the flowerprint house   dress of late morning the long jeans

of the afternoon   cantillations of the kimono angry strips of
fetish in the popular   black standing at midnight between us
holy and pulsating   our linked haiku tearing   out of the
void attacking with the full weight of our light

PSALM

The atom of all   blond adam who flies   above the ruts of this
age without sleep and sleeps   in the broken walled cracks
in my brow in the arrogant corner   of my pride   scatter of
unkempt atoms planging guitar notes of atom   myself re-
visited unsore   little prince joggling the whole   galaxy
with one lob   of the worlds ball stitched to the glove of
love little fellow   accomplice   Kid Cupid & Chocolate together   sweet tooth for this rotting   old mouth   bright
almond eyed innocence   first bud of belly   last buddy before dark prophet of fungs   easy love   simple quiet fierce
      joke angry breakup of domination into   an 8X8 laugh-
ter   hardly begun and already outliving the compass points
started   weather veins whirring   who is rising   I am
sinking   who is yawning   I am sunk worshipfully your
old lord ship   who is dawning out of pitchblende   orphic
radium David   all harps and hearts turned to   the sun

SOUTHWEST IKON

What rice Juarez   questionmock   we go down   to the
blue paddies between the thighs   this year   sixtynine
what chop sticks those skinny legs   put the black   curtain
over the head lines what   victory what   survival   questionmock   her body scribbled across   the wall of the war
of the skull   fifteen years old   me and my friend Jim
step out of the picture   turn the corner for a cup   coffee
what   color   questionmock

20

PASSETEMPO

I work in the dark   behind I gauge out a cafe   of wrists
chained or cut   bleeding a knife sharp enough for   your
tongue   my finger the bites of Bavarian   teeth the aviatrix
     along the coccyx of dreams where were one obscenery
done and undone   you lie   back you turn over my kisses
     drip wet after rain   of pat pleasure   slaphappy kicks for
good   measure of rod   you surround with the mouth   of
your eye ball   theater of nibbles   that you treat dutch
tulipping like the kyriaki of the greek like   the dodecaphonic
boot   like soho in summery machine   all the books of the
world all the poems   and still room for your mouth   that
wants what will come   in a minute shell be rising from sea
sound kept hidden   by ducts under tissue   in pieces of
organ the animal other   ours   hers   together   split
my inner cunt spiration   your wildest spit hair   is rising
spread   is standing outside   the astral leer over   your
rump riding spurs   swallow me whole root and raw leave me
     empty to fill   oui us   with her nighthorn   virgin
animal is letting down her hair is stepping out   of her blue
humiliation is fixing the wooden   jesus there is my green
fire in her teeth there is your green fire in her eyes   blazing
down into shoulder   as you pour into me   mine as I hail
     with cries as she stretches   out lies lapping our eyelids
with the tail swishing flick   of her tongue tipped with incense
all the softly glittering desiderata long

DEATHMASK

All climates broken fragments   the dinghy cut loose   of
space marionetted to the music   of deadly containment
uptight and black owning the nights small business   I drive
through on wheels   to the soul sound of engine you are
waiting to connect with   trouble called The Man I keep at
seventeen   stymies under the apocalyptic clear skin of a sun of
     a gun or bitch of a belt hitched   up over the border from
Tijuana with a leer   in the belly where I see   myself
mockery on trial top and bottom   the fall in in a roll   down
to the bare nakedness only another   onionring of conspiracy

crawling out of the bed of assassinated   Jerusalem is in
tact   desert bullets fly all over the minds technocracy   a
grid settles between words   old bride unseasonable unnatural
indignation   two cups of coffee for the price of one Sirhan
Sirhan   the distances rising to the shape   of what already
has blown the top   off the skull   crawling always centi-
pedally to Paris where   in leech spring all   return to go
acynicling

CHOPPT

Animal I come out   of this small place called   Edom
without knowing anything called Edom   anywhere before the
kings died   by my hand on a gun called the modern truths
know only it was lie   and stand still and see the sails   free
on the water   the birds in the air   whoever you you broken
and   split you division you incapacity to   answer that you
are they are   at once and all connected   up with your maid
your mad scheme   to permit me continue   dreaming in
your wet arms

DES

You away you in here   knife after night so   clear to the
bone your laugh the rafters of   our shambles shake and pro-
nounce   our white teeth pink gums   the animals supple
    fury in the suns   new pride the letters the song   oh dove
my undefiled   oh black bird dipt into the pure continent of
    sound changes   the olive of Yod   taste our long range
    the color of giraffic laughter   along the winding neck of the
Zomba   where love and fear take root   fingernails take
each other   by the heart for the walk into

STAINEDGLASS

These furious things these night invasions   always when I
want sleep never wanting   to sleep wanting   you

22

would lock me up in here   make up all the poems   amounting to nothing   innunendi   infinitely variable   by the
ocean where we are   a couple of skins   bawded and still
   she bears us steady steady on making mountains of visions of
the waves   giving back the last dancing asias   the last
magical distances   with the eldest taste and first salt   and
deadsea smegma   in which we drink and roll browning selves
in the sand turning bread standing   leavened in the oven of
each   new sun

LIGAMENT

Cobra of black   coming snake of Zayen   hieroglyph of
instinct more powerful than words we have become   a dead
mouse   our little arms and legs tucked under   the cobra
slithers   forward through the rock and twig setting   in this
cage behind glass   in the gardens   his length rising to his
head   above us lordly   bestial his depths beginning to open
       from the end of him to   his mouth   never were we at
the height of our speed   so lordly   his jaws expanding a
massively quiet violence   without bound

BEARD

Straw napkins and this closed   cerrado joint about a half
mile from the Pacific where its clear   bondage and your
mouth full of   thongs   and hurt waits for or does it after
so many years   while I still manufacture the poem of   the
wooden box between your legs   the one between my eyes
full of the law   which is this   you I walk around without
       ever touching through all   the slime and dirty troughs I
stick something or other   into as well as these blackeyed
seasons green is   what I once called   grass when young and
larger   ran then through   the grass was where I dont
remember sprawling   in meditation your eyes are the color
   of grass and the sharp edges   your hair the way it breaks in
two   your mouth   that silencer I reach for my vest suddenly studded   with dear life your thongs around every movement   limp me back in   an old scandal of a sandal   and
clouts for the other guy foot

STAVE

A blinding light of October   here on stone   houses at
worlds end smithereens flying me back   through iridescence
to the island where all messages were   transmitted with the
pain   of light entering a dark place exploding   apollonial
fragments in a gemmy house called   the broken head of the
small world   scattered throughout the four seasons   of the
I Ching attainment of Nada   more than a grave body and
grace   there is in old and old again   and older still than
there or here   I stretch this girls mind half naked on the
sand   beside the great sea side and sentence you to write end-
lessly   the infinite variations   the same

THE SHEKINA

So is this body devoured   by her who is you   my ribs drip
with the black juice of her   bitterest olives   the butterfly
strikes the heart of the dew into colors   across the dome of
the morning mind   who can come in unto when the war is
heavy   round the feet and heart goes on all fours   mouth
has been declared backwards I go after her she   comes to-
ward and it is   dreaming in a card with a dog and a crab and
the moon   and it is   a game in the jackets of asylum

I went to the end   of the house and found you   in the corner you sprawled inside me   death was yours unrolling   its
long dark hair the gaze I would crush   with my feet if they
werent   spiked to the times   and where wine should have
burst I   simply drink in the raucous bud she begins to gather
    in the drowning of the whores of l'esprit she rises dresses to
be   more naked   she sets aside all wounds like the piece-
meal fabric   she will be used   for ascension happily

You are what she wears through   my garments for you are
    the stroke within   the apples turning in the night   the
pulled stems   slow devolution of flesh on the   broadside of
passive revolt   with the indissoluble leather   flowers of the
night   with sweet concentration barbs of   mesh stockings
tasting of   incense and travestys eggs whipped   with blood

24

with menstruations of Jerusalem wrapped in lamentations
    dark strings of the song of crux   pinch of jasmine and
jade   knuckles of a thunder faroff

Now we are totally   instrumental   now movement is
ritualized by the dream of you now   even command is ren-
dered a plea   barks go down the apocalyptic spine of   our
fusion on their knees   everything lipped and tongued
everything moistened by wings of the delerious bees riding the
dark rivers   bursting with plantations   and the deep fuck
and the cunt   of our cries are gathered   letter by letter
into the serene nod   rising as it rains   all over our peace

MIXTURE

You can always tell   nothing is happening   by the way
    time flies and weighs Galya says   no pounds with wings
    her brushes are that way when   for instance   she is
painting layers   of space the apron of the butcher   in
Chicago flaying   the meat she couldn't look at   being   a
window she made a notation of   opening it twenty years to
    the day today   meaning your eyes

JOHN

Loves letters to selfs notes   music which is at the root
brother blue how tenderly Tibet doth   rain the soft gongs in
    the night ending any way going on   page by page   in-
defineably as   Londinium   is in here a place where once
we met   simple to when the darkness   fell and all engaged
the cruel   offering of alphabets running on without purpose
and having no body to speak of   this dome this cranial fault
    this atomic place breathing in breathing out   wings in-
dependent of birds abstract as concrete   in flight as doves of
sounding grace   notes spoken for after it was You   after
all who tells the story   by rote through me your letting go
    of things unimaginable   whose town this is the soft com-
posure of   then in the night when in the night we breathe
vapors upward of winderful   thungs bursting   relative to
summer spoken for in spring   govindas

VENICE

This kiss of my own black   heel and spike plunged into   a
panic of the mouth of a siren   scream along the arm of the
boulevard   gratuitous with trees whipping   the seams un-
stable in the back   seat careening through   nights pumped
with impotent leather   seeds raising a tender   travesty in
the sky   aborting stars along the premier screw socketed into
the throat   eroding dreams down the foetal eyes of the needle
stitching into the shuddering   vain heart on the end of the
pier   into this ocean without water

MOIST

This flutter of abashed   kimono belted with haikai and blue
   plums of a peacock tail spattering   the night I lifted up and
kissed moist indignations of a whirling   disk sighing all the
way   down to Po River between   the banks of a hungry
necessity broken fingers into a wilderness of animals running out
   of your nails writing allover my back   the scroll wilder
than any sea   son penned by me any mountain   climbed
by my mouth   or sleep I might have dreamed any south
flying bird

SYBLINK

Her lips opening   and closing between my eyes   the movement closing opening to my wildest   terror of how she
birthed me this dark   earth wear and   tear of the veil
   for the rich rivering gyzm to   behold for the deep super-
fice to   explode between thieves   her lips opening and closing her tongue slithering   along the chap   terranean skin
forked and lizard   dreaming of stallion   cry   of whale
shoot conceiving the mandrill hyena and cock   crow long and
shrill   the aieeee of being human orgasmic devilish godly shell
cracking   egg face horrible and bleeding animal poor dervish
   of the wounds I look into   you   the fairest of fall

26

TORC

But feeling by chafe   feeling between always black   and
blue electric fricative   sick but feeling besides never   clear
through to the absolute There   feeling war down the raw side
of the cheek   where she scratched for air the cancer   of
cities spreading throughout   the pancreas nailed to a Two
    hung up on one   die-cut   book slapping each cheek and
so deep she lies   in you the dark   amazement working
this long distant call   from one braid to the other   pinned
suddenly to   one side of memory   eroding into dawn
two white birds breaking from your left breast   egg on my
dreams   ecologies shaping the dunes   of the morning where
I lie   face down among these stars of clear   blindness
braille to be tasted   dry bread of day draped in the white
gown of morning without you   to frighten   to and

BANTAM

The fire contained the mouth   put to sleep the level   of lips
your finger upon   the way you guide me with desire   gone
yet this unnameable liason song   that continues into the others
    night in the small room   across your body flung
stupid and popular dirty with war and boots why   don't you
ever curse how high   was butter   I lick the cow from your
thigh eat   the furious dream

CHAIR

I have only to sit and I burn   beside you the planets   in my
skull grew small as you are all   inundation of the vessel
of air holding the key to my going out   alone   individual
    meaning nothing walking beside you under the stars   you
plant your tides your quartermoony inspirations   east and
west in each nostrils   swooping up and all the scattered
disciplines called war   fruitless drops in the bucket of your
big tear

NOBODADDY

Silence   oh gentle girl the guns   make me see and all
compadres the world   as the little daughter does   stroke
her big cat Chopin in the sun

CLAY

Old friend of many   sudden stupidities between   us and
the dull middle west of beginning   young is the song at last
youre in the fold of my flowering age turned inward   and full
of the violences   of far distances cries and reproaches
never never answered   save by what is word and beast   of
poem in your mouth shoved   for all the fists we asked of each
other   for all the hates we loved   too much to bruise

VISTULA

Against the word   war against myselves   you   against
a destiny of dead music   born in the cunt of the contra
anew   in the fall of the land and I   nothing less than
another it   tangled by shock wires bombed by electric   at-
tacks of abbreviations numbers   of greeks a bullion stew of
gold   offerings   a graveyard of rubber tubings where the
glottal stopped against your mouth   viciously beautiful
against your thigh passive   for thrust against   the inner
lesson of your deep school amounting   to bucks and bucks
    and a pile of come with hair   and a mountain of doom with
teeth   against your shoulder sweet auschwitz   into the
pit   your arm against the lens with this shattered glass
against the poem with   the mess of this sigh against her eyes
against yours   her nails against my side   yours driven
through   the other   against the hiss and dinch of the long
cigaret of stud of star married   to the split infinitive
tense of the morning lap of the black milk dog

SPATIAL

These beings across   my gaze and then   within these angels
I want out outside put them set them a   part at arms length
hold them with hold them for   Gods sake the balance   this
flow   blinding with light they come storming   offering help
one   does one   need being dead seeing clear   through
and through   things   the light form of them the wing
spans the way they are   eating the air of me beating by ocean
at end on the sand at the tent   fire   the moon slivver these
quivverings   shudders these   dwindlings now   deep
blue these veins running out of a hand   who to vermillion
    diminishing the bits of a teaching leaving   these shells

USA

Without my voice   keeping on   urging the sun   his peg
goes limp that vague   glaze comes over   which later on
could   harden into dead nuls of an ism   racked with bullets
aimed   at the temple intent on keeping   his voice with
in

VISCERAL

Fist of an anguspur   ripped through a tonsil   torching this
cry where the sand gathers   dunework for the Doublenix
    where the open psalm draws   cuts in the river   burst
spit of war and her   body up tight twice for good   measure
the funnybone aboli in the sunlight sleep pommelled royal blue
    mitts   to wake up the face punched with all the old angers
        with the truss of the hip   jock in the jackrabbit night
with no one opposite everyone   in fighting free   and its
come to me gone one   here in this room where   all is done
over and over is browned and charred stiff   animal of seven
dead kisses   hearse of my words   poor boxing ptyx and
deadly   dumb wind blowing through the shack of the world
    nobody possesses   anything possessively   no soul ob-

29

sessing no   thung   but tongues ten times breaking
silent in the center of the room   full of edible shoes   spank
shine

CHANTAGE

The street bottom   of this throat rammed with   banana
dildoes   hot dog of poetry eaten   whole by the mustard
blast self   and still you keep coming you keep   affirming a
body a faith   I lie hard by   letters of a black   law
sparks of fire   urn in darkness   wind blown through the
hair of your flame bending   over burning within the cool
heart beat eaten whole   sipping the sometimes   that I feel
      you as you not me without   me outside me   in a place
somewhere   theres rain and fall on your face   and your
lips do not care   being wet being free   for the moment I am

TURNING

With a blaze of pain with   body's last fire O   keanos great
god mother of all yet   masculine gendered   steady and
driving I begin the approach   all fire seeming   superfluous
drop   too me superfluous superfluous   words   one hand
full of sand one with a gull   Okeanos billowing   Okeanos
with sails   dinch of a cigaret   33 years long   this wave
in the sun leftover

THEORPHRASTUS

With cuffs three inches too wide   either side of hairless bone
legs socks curled over   unkempt lip   what do you want
man   I got a million piled up inside   some with shaved
heads so close   to the magical bone   you can read the lay-
out of auschwitz   hear the xylophone nachtmusik   the ribs
make clanking around   in the pits   of my eyes around midnight the kids hugged so close   they go right through the
mother rag   lie inbetween whats left of the dug ikons of Not

30

foetal defuncts   acres of masses of   what if only were
butterflies   and the Thung could end with a shot of cherry-
blossoms bursting on the spring vein   branch against the sky
     if only   but he keeps on spitting his lice   he goes on
warping   the rag he doesnt give a fuck about my images
hes got a million dirty ones of his own   we can shuffle the
deck starting nine can play   Hitler Better or Black   fart
cigars with coffee served dumb   by a succubus bra   out of
old helmets and bungs with Zenith nostalgias   with prelimi-
nary tales   with mainevent fungoes   a jigger of   hell
whats a jigger of   what the hell is a jigger of spit doing under
my eyes   dig the deadly provincial time leaning back kicking
out the electric   guitar as he falls on his head breaking into a
lot   of hooey with mitts   keeping tawdry eye on the cross
to see she dont   altogether limp to the absolute heels of the
death boobyprize   coughed up in lieu of grass   going twenty
reactions too quick   in a jag at a meal   and wears sex like
a snarl pointing nowhere   connotations stopped dumb   in
the tracks of a science thats organized dreams into unions
of ticking alarms   and your croak and mine are only stunt
men   doing turns in a black   tree where the leaves already
have fallen   naked were late   fall ridiculous shivering cold
and snow comes in   big flapping footprints   one for you
one for me when   the clubby mace falls either way

TABLET

So then   it is What   returns us to this meeting   here
which always says thanks   be within the hurt   that
brought me round   brings me to the small dignity   I fear
and fight   the mechanism of   so much infinite   drawing
you   across years   losing steadily with the downward smile
of   style

WHISPER

And declare nothing   let it be a spoken   this be done be
what it will finis now be   gin again a   leph hardly a
breath in tact   discreetly within limits like   she insists it
be   like naturally   nature

ECTO

The snail is taking centuries through   the atom of my mind
now   the earth is broken it   will be I see slowly   all
right by turns instead of burnings   of the day instead of night
     with a sun equal to the grain of hebrew trillions on the
sand   the teeth czeching all over again the hair crazy rou-
manian on both sides   of the fallen curtain face   one cross
of cocks in the stall of the pride   cocktails for the race of
gotham

BOOTS

Come with me up   bawd mountain crest in the moon   fallen
with wars double   affronting pressure   now soft now hard
     on the furious virgin flinging   her two timing gear
leer and suicide   out of our young tough night   into the
dawn grey   rumple of khacki   song

PACIFIC

You I approach   dumb as I walked out   once on the sand
dripping blood with a slap   for good measure   and pray
you   whom I lost when I ran through a city   and allover
the electric   world with a will bent   by nails into changes
     you all this   last winter waiting for the last   fling of
words at the games   in the grooves of the wars decay I walk
     these last beads of   sweat this May day   down the last
dry dune where I played   dead to fly back to this wet   beginning

WIPEOUT

You force   nothing sleeps between   your legs you smile
aversion handing out your double   the ocean turns into
the meadow of her body plunged by all my dividing   stukas
     her chin turns rubbery away chafing kisses   promises of
hatred she will bring you   later a dream of meat you will share
     in the bone inflamed night passed between you   my peace
exchanging nothing   its only the hat trick   with wigs
switched like lights with   smiles upturned down   for the
love of some fiction that raves   for the bark of a dog returning   you to the smell of yourself   in the gutter   running
down the sky a streak of mint green lightning   judgment of
facts I am   at the end and stuffed into the middle   east of
nowhere and west to the dead   head sea gone to ash   with
the kiss   hissing sound of   the cigaret dying and lights
out   and privacy grows   a threepart   tight boot of a
land stretching allover   the bed of the bawds   beginning to
feel and now wanting to die   every drag

LATITUDE

The numbered silver   of the radium of   the congregation
mindbent thumbs hanging on   the letters of wars   lord
law   come with me the golden dance   of vowels round
the fivepointed star   the sixsided teaching   of shithouse
graffiti   on their knees   in the twilight come white and
black   stuffings of the heart   beat eaten swing through my
mouth   little beloved   through the rotten sixtyeight and
nine   of this pressured millenial   this metaphysical point
of a bullet   fired through the park   ferocious with idiot
spinnings of a disk back   to the first lie   told with the slap
and cry shaking the junk   upsidedown before christ   in the
first rain of blood and blond   faith growing through all vain
     glorious atoms of Hemo streaming   down the shot streets
with the oldest song first vibration in the gut   stands up the
tree   bursts new apostles of dirty leaves   on your lids open
     for love to the many of mizrahim   is cool laughter all
around the cycles   of Edom who will roll back home when
     she comes through the last   bars with her arms singing

victory   Daughter oh Daughter   walk my arm to the sea
that is rotten and old   bring it back to me wet   lift it up
to me new each dawn blue and green   here where we run
pungent with juice of plum inking the sand   with hand over
      hand of this real stuff   of son and the daughter   of
joy flashing down   east to tell we all saw your father suicided
      smile calling himself Mozart   a small boy running
through footprinted   notes of his airs   in the sky over
junks and buff catamarans   with a thin bend of   play of
eternaday growing big in the bellies   of our eyes   where
lovers meet at the fierce of their gall   in the sunlit afternoon
risen above   the dark mourning waves melodious coffins
touching at the firs   in the fist of our throat clenched   at
the edge bursting from under   a high noon there lies our in-
sane to be   free to be slave with a stone   heart after heart
till the pyramids done   the winged things closed and night
again real   scent of their bodies   rose no way but the waves
now the strange has been ridden   the dike fingered through
the androgyne joke of a war gone   to grass burning black
      fire in the hair cut short the little bow   blue and the story
old as the rap   out of the side spurting mouths   lying in
the gutter   my three brains scattered through the five
boroughs of gropes for   a slovvenly brother who would teach
me   the wrongs would lead me back   tight up the dune
down to   the water curbed son of a sneer   crown of my
curly master   in this slum of torn stockings running   with
black humor wrapped around my neck   the franc note at the
tip   of my tongue whipping sighs from deaths organ
tousels of genius conductor of volt age crowning of the peer
      sidesplitting laughs and viced   strokes kill daughter and
kill out   the old burns in with   new hells bell bottom world
turning up   with enough for the other with   young and
old dogs in the back   washed speedway where   we move
through the hers and the hymns of the trees   black and gold
at the end   of the night mare in the soft ram   of dreams
      speak to the risen passive tense in the incense   dark shy
birds of all oil   a lordship ever surfaced for   circle the
slick talk to the milkfall   from the high arch of the heel you
are   who spoke through the various   goatskin media
who sent the dollar to the donut factory   sat me lowdown in
Olivias Cafe   taught me the names of the 26 streets for the
blue balls rolling home cherry   26 cuts and humbles washed
by the whip of your dark   26 letters of the law in   the war
of the public gun   26 bends and barbs wired to the paranoic
congregation   26 not 22 2 for me   6 for you and all   the
blows of your hallucination   and translation of my   occult

34

alchemical dream of birth   under switched hats and the gaze
   of your simple leather   apron in front of the Cafe Rue de
la Paix   the road through the Interchange   the stretch
from the center to the sea   changing into the whole   heart
of the angel

IN PRAISE

That is memoriam   this voice raised just a step   above the
level that is no reach   for death still goes a foot ahead   of
the depths and a mighty   fine inch higher than the   grass
naming object   so deep in you cannot have cannot   possess
this moment   immediate cannot is this   not but to halve
   the story is   later and then is walking alone long after
is over at dusk   heading into   the closing of the sun   in
memoriam   that is this   dark with stars faintly wide with
space gently   listening

INTERKNIT

Melody older without   comparison strain of   messiah re-
laxing the tense all   bursts in folded like leaves   the night
of the beard of the rabbi studded with Alephs   I sleep in
the song of a dream of a song I am   dreaming Egyptians
dropping   like flies I carry their eyes home to Jerusalem
wail at the wall for the Way the old new will meet and now
      dawns in the long throat her brave suppling   bird final
nun

DOWNWIND

What Jim and I share   in this Ground Zero   walkup over
a veteran boulevard the memory   of posed and paid-for
realisms of your long black life   of hair stretching from the
dead   center of your body framed in   a braided intertwist
      with a box of hemp tied round this red   nazi song of
extreme   children stuck in the middle of the night fantastic

if only to round a round timbre   a cup of old voluptuous-
ness make of   your breast that these hands   might palm
off one last contour before   the cool turns absolutely
leather pictures having made us   what we are pictures having
     poured into the afternoon   bored eyes of the   genera-
tion flickers with what prophetics you are   broken up into
these studs of flesh scattered mosaic outside the law   stunning
after all shock   has won the goddess space   untouchable

Z.

Then there was no hurry no longer   rush light   no place to
have to get to no one   believe this worry   home   was
exile and is   the rest this long jew   I carry as I marry
the day with the night in   sight

DAVID

Dune of me   hand in me   eye desert sun   the tribes
moving through shadows of the lashes   count up to millenial
     count down to the sea where he comes riding   waves of
his cockhappy   rocket with a cross held aloft with the smile
     of a boy changed by asia   who talks rain bows breaking
out   in a rash of   of the flashing   dusky cupids allover
the is   realizable swirls of the sands

CLEF

Strange chain I have   by low melodic   made of a wrist so
     easily breakable see   in your town I come into   my
form which is   her being free and all   my arm across her
     belly the other perpendicular with a cigaret my long dark
hair   good enough for three

ATOMIC TRASH TORA

Almost the lyric   body swung over the shoulder   of the
limey at Dachau and dumped   into pit with the other
lovely emaciations after so many years as she had life   and to-
ward the end of the war on Pico Boulevard in Mister Teas
ressurrected she lives with the music that is going   to go on
forever you   motherfucking swine   she stands up there
eyes   utterly glazed between lashes rubber over nipples
sequined dypsobelt at the crotch   in love and giving back to
the box   its due flesh   and into your two faces the double-
kissed waggle   clearing the head of desecrations   putting
her long black hair   in the line of your gun swivelling   in
your terror absolutely   present in death   and giving not a
fuck but to Johnny Dildo   who she kisses   bleeding between the sheets   stacked with eyes I am   two of them
am two of you you warrior brother bastard theres not a jew
in christendom but hes dead nor   a christian in America but
hes cunted   at sound speed   every minute muffing back
down to the gawk   in the tissue that wakes   up the old bag
of urine   running everyday from gunpoint   wild and
beaten and throwing it way with a snarl   my man shes no pro
fessional big assed couple of mountains giving birth   to a
blue veined humiliation in your face shes here   by grace of
god shes working the night and if you give her Mozart shell
swivel the same   or turn her on Webern her crotch will
chafe diamonds   to pay back your leers with the bone of her
savage submission   and heres where I find the law   of the
dead fat book closed   balance attained here   in the syna-
gogue of gape and a kiki   no warmer than lamed   where I
stop short of death   and die into a nasty bunch of syllables
called   the tribe of Israel oh wear me like the idiot raving this
is   wear me as your black star sabbath your hat your hidden
suspenders made in Damascus   lay me on the motel table
on the cards of your tarot   on the pontiac dashboard   in
the hip   pocketbook of your crawl   I be her law   her
dark hair her engine of orifices stuffed   with the screaming
cocks of the orgy   pennies flung from every where   nickles
and dimes of laughter worthy of the Dipper   and better be-
cause we crawl with lap gnash we bite synoptic   rich with the
devil   poor as gods sweet   piss spattering the lines   of
the tracks of this desert   wasteland from apocalypse to the
genetic back   singing internationale of low spines and nelly
dances   all

DIAFRAM

Deathly mostly timely   or wobbling between   the blood
running money just under the streets flesh   and the light tra-
dition gone   fluorescent on formica   juked music picked
from the teeth of a faint   girl who isnt sure she wasnt
spiked in the eye   scared of the arm after   seeing what
palooka of a christ   the underjunk makes with   its black
with its leathery tip   peasant heel in the provincial   bigcity
rough fraud of an odor of the farm   and theres your Holy
Yod and theres   the tetractys of your dactyl   crawling
around you quack   wherever this little rue turns wherever
this narrow street   between a couple of bum   dreams
wherever this avenue zipped up behind   as long as that one
three   inches high and that other making two   into 11 at
midnight   at the corner of Dancers Muscle and Stompers Calf
     where the ankle bracelet of puberty asks my brand with her
tongue   my teeth my kiss my bite   up the ruffled giggle
     come music of Lautre & Amont   into the black and tan
flickers again of small parks   of benches and pee lonely
ravens of the borough brushing my hair with failure   of the
first pressed   crotch to crotch against the wall   of Labia
Minor   is you I am after   prying open the little lid of death
     box between my eyes   opening our rabbinically rolling
scroll writ with hickies   hanging down the long ridiculously
religiously doggy   tung

CROWN

Your face I do not want   remembering the blinding stand
radiant girl in the Hampstead station   en route to Jerusalem
     was there so much light   in the western world
mothers and daughters walked arm in arm allover the heath
to a man

CHILD TWO

Sometimes we shall go   to wide commons and see   no trees
nor any houses and heaths   where there is hardly grass
the caterpillar whispered to   his other end   burst with
laughable sadness   when he looked upon   the wings that
went   over and over all   with meadows falling green
and suns so many drinking   out of the godly bowl

AN EDITION OF
FOUR HUNDRED COPIES
HAS BEEN PRINTED AT
CHRISTOPHER'S PRESS,
SANTA BARBARA,
FOR TREE BOOKS,
BOLINAS,
MAY 1971.

FRONTISPIECE BY THE AUTHOR
AND DESIGN BY M. MAYTAG,
COMPOSITION BY YOUNG &
MACKINTOSH, PRESSWORK
BY G. ALBERS.

TREE BOOKS